What's for Lunch?

How Schoolchildren Eat around the World

Written by **Andrea Curtis**

Photography by **Yvonne Duivenvoorden**

To the good people everywhere working to make school lunch equitable, healthy, and gentle on the earth—A.C.

Acknowledgments

Thanks are due to a host of people all over the world, whose dedication to children and food justice inspired this book, and whose careful reading ensured it makes sense. Photographer Yvonne Duivenvoorden, illustrator Sophie Casson, and designer Karen Powers made the words come to life. Jackie Kaiser saw the potential right away, and Karen Li shepherded it through the process with wisdom, care, and a generous dollop of fun. Peter Carver and Richard Dionne gave the book a warm welcome and a happy new home. Finally, thanks and love to Nick Saul—whose dedication to healthy food for all is without compare—and our boys, Ben and Quinn, who good-naturedly put up with nonstop food talk.

Yvonne would like to thank food stylist Lucie Richard for her help and expertise throughout this project. Also, a big thank-you to producer Sarah Lichter for her invaluable services.

Published by Red Deer Press, A Fitzhenry & Whiteside Company
195 Allstate Parkway, Markham, ON, L3R 4T8
www.reddeerpress.com

Published in the United States by Red Deer Press, A Fitzhenry & Whiteside Company
311 Washington Street, Brighton, Massachusetts, 02135

Edited for the Press by Peter Carver
Cover design by Daniel Choi & Karen Powers
Illustrations by Sophie Casson

Printed and bound in China

5 4 3 2

We acknowledge with thanks the Canada Council for the Arts, and the Ontario Arts Council for their support of our publishing program. We acknowledge the financial support of the Government of Canada through the Canada Book Fund (CBF) for our publishing activities.

ONTARIO ARTS COUNCIL
CONSEIL DES ARTS DE L'ONTARI

Canada Council
for the Arts
Conseil des Arts
du Canada

Library and Archives Canada Cataloguing in Publication
Curtis, Andrea
What's for lunch? / Andrea Curtis ; Yvonne Duivenvoorden, photographer.
ISBN 978-0-88995-482-3
1. School children--Food--Juvenile literature. I. Title.
LB3475.C87 2012   j371.7'16   C2012-901543-1

Publisher Cataloging-in-Publication Data (U.S)
Curtis, Andrea.
What's for lunch? / Andrea Curtis ; Yvonne Duivenvoorden.
[   ] p. : col. photos. ; cm.
Summary: An examination of the food consumption by school children in thirteen countries; focusing on school lunches, as well as the inequality of food and the importance of healthy, nutritious food.
ISBN: 978-0-88995-482-3 (pbk.)
1. School children – Nutrition – Juvenile literature. 2. Children – Nutrition – Juvenile literature.   I. Duivenvoorden, Yvonne. II. Title.
371.716 dc23   LB3473.C878 2012

Contents

Every day, all over the world,
children eat together at school.

In Tanzania, a teacher hits a rock against a rusty metal tire rim hanging from a tree, and the loud clanging calls the students outside to share their meal. In Canada, the buzz of a bell over a loudspeaker sends kids racing for the gymnasium where tables are set up for a busy, noisy lunch.

Whether their school is under the vast umbrella of a banyan tree, in a dusty tent held up with poles, or in a sturdy brick structure in the heart of a bustling city, all children need a healthy lunch to be able to learn and grow. Good food nourishes both our bodies and our brains. It's one of the basic building blocks of life.

As the world has become more interconnected, what we eat has become part of a huge complex global system. Food is now the biggest industry on Earth. Growing it, processing it, transporting it, and selling it has a major impact on people and the planet. Unpack a school lunch, and you'll discover that food is connected to issues that matter to everyone—things such as climate change, health, and inequality.

There are some children, for instance, who have nothing to eat at home. War, displacement, poverty, and natural disasters cause sixty-six million kids around the world to go to school hungry every day. For some of these students, free school lunch programs are a lifeline. Once they have eaten, they can concentrate on their lessons. Their health improves, and they have a fighting chance to build a better future for themselves and their families.

Other kids have enough to eat, but their food—including the lunch provided at school—isn't healthy, and they are overweight or obese. More than a billion people around the world—many of them schoolchildren—are overweight and face serious diet-related illnesses such as diabetes, heart disease, and some types of cancer.

What kids eat for school lunch can also tell us a lot about the culture and history that make them and their country unique. After all, what better way to get to know people than to share a meal with them? Everywhere you look, there's a kaleidoscope of colors, surprising and delicious foods, and inspiring stories to discover. Kids are gardening, cooking, and speaking out about their right to eat healthy lunches. Their work is transforming schools and helping the planet, too.

So come have a peek in the lunch boxes, bowls, trays, and mugs of children around the world. You'll be surprised at just how much you can learn by seeing what other kids eat for school lunch.

Tokyo, Japan

Five schoolchildren stand behind a long table at the front of their classroom in Tokyo, Japan. They're wearing crisp white caps, aprons, and masks that cover their noses and mouths, and they're holding big spoons ready to ladle out the day's lunch. Their classmates line up to be served today's menu of miso soup and grilled mackerel with rice. Sometimes there's an orange or apple for dessert, and there's always milk to drink. Unless students have allergies, they aren't offered a choice; they're expected to eat the healthy meal made in the school kitchen.

Before beginning to eat, everyone must wait until the day's servers have their food and have taken their seats. The children lay out their cloth placemats and set their chopsticks neatly at the top of the mats. (By about age five, Japanese children can use chopsticks with ease.) Then, with their hands clasped in front of them, the children chant in unison, "Itadakimasu" [ee-tah-**day**-kee-mass-soo]. This means "Let's eat!" and is a thank-you to those who have provided the meal.

Beginning in elementary school and continuing into junior high, all students take part in school lunch, called *kyushoku* [kai-u-**shoh**-kyoo]. Even teachers and the principal join in, sitting with the children in their classrooms. Eating together and enjoying the same food is an essential part of the meal. The respect, manners, and cleanliness practiced here are as important as math or gym class. At the end of *kyushoku*, the children once again offer their thanks, saying, *"Gochisosama deshita"* [**goh**-chee-soh-sah-mah day-**shee**-tah], meaning "That was quite a feast!"

Before going outside to play, everyone pitches in to clean up the classroom and return the food and dishes to the kitchen. Most Japanese schools don't even have a caretaker because the students work hard to keep their classes and the hallways clean.

1 Worried about reports that Japanese children are losing touch with their culture and traditions, one high school has put a chopstick skills test on its entrance exam. Applicants must be able to move everything from beans and dice to marbles from one plate to another!

2 The monthly menu for *kyushoku* is given to children and parents in advance. It includes a breakdown of the nutritional value and calories in the ingredients, plus information about where the produce was grown and how particular ingredients, such as the healthy seaweed and tofu in this miso soup, will benefit students.

3 Japan is an island nation, and kids here eat nearly their weight in seafood every year. Mackerel, salmon, and sardines are common, and whale meat—a traditional food considered rich in protein—has been reintroduced in some school lunches. Although commercial whaling was banned in 1986 to protect endangered species, Japan still kills some whales for research. The meat is used by the Japanese government for school lunches, served as burgers or fried in breadcrumbs.

4 Once one of the healthiest nations in the world, Japan is seeing rising rates of obesity and diet-related illnesses such as diabetes. Like elsewhere in the world, the traditional diet is changing as Western foods such as hamburgers and french fries are introduced. Although rice is still an important staple, Japanese children today eat only half the rice in a year that their grandparents did in the early 1960s.

Lucknow, India

Women from a local community group have been working in the heat of the kitchen all morning. They're preparing the midday meal at this small public school outside the city of Lucknow in northern India. They scoop out a lunch of rice and curried lentils from a big metal serving pot, offering it to the children who line up. Some children carry plates or bowls brought from home; those who can't afford plates hold out small blackboards or notebooks covered with a sheet of paper to receive their food.

The children take their meal outside, where they squat on the ground in the schoolyard and eat with their hands. Many Indian people say food tastes better eaten with your fingers. But it's important that only the right hand is used for touching food; the left is reserved for use in the bathroom.

Public schools in India offer a free lunch to all children up to age fourteen. For many of these kids, it's the only meal they will eat all day. Although the country's economy has grown in recent years, two hundred and thirty million people still go hungry on a daily basis—more than in any other place in the world. Every day, two thousand to three thousand Indian children die as a result of malnutrition.

But the "midday meal scheme," as school lunch is known in India, does more than fill bellies; it also helps increase attendance and improve literacy. Poor families are more likely to send their children to school if they are guaranteed a meal. Indian girls, who are often expected to work for their families from a very young age, especially benefit from this. Families can better afford to send their daughters to get an education—and go without their labor—if they are fed at school.

1 You've probably noticed there aren't any vegetables in this lunch. Although veggies are supposed to be included in every midday meal, schools rely on irregular funding and often can't afford to buy them. Despite the free lunch, nearly 70% of young Indian children suffer from anemia, a condition caused in part by a lack of iron-rich foods such as greens and beans. When you are anemic, it's hard to concentrate and your memory doesn't work well. You feel tired, have headaches and can't handle physical activity.

2 Known as *dal,* this dish of lentils or peas cooked with spices is one of the most common meals in India. *Dal* is an excellent vegetarian source of protein, iron, and fiber, ideal for the 80% of Indian people who are followers of the Hindu faith and do not eat meat. Cows are considered sacred creatures to Hindus, and they are allowed to wander wherever they like on the streets of many villages.

3 Supporters of the midday meal scheme say it encourages equality in this country of extreme wealth and extreme poverty. The idea is that when children talk to one another over a shared meal, things such as where you come from and who your parents are don't matter as much. The government also recommends that kitchen staff be members of India's most impoverished groups. This helps provide work and eliminate discrimination.

2 ▽

1 ▷

◁ 3

9

Nantes, France

The lunchroom in this Loire Valley school is decorated with colorful murals and artwork that hangs from the ceiling. It hums with the chatter of children who sit in small groups around circular tables while they enjoy their four-course school lunch.

The midday meal is made from scratch in the school kitchen by trained chefs using fresh produce (bought locally if possible). Lunch begins with a choice of salad—maybe butter lettuce with smoked duck—followed by roast chicken or fish with vegetables, then a cheese course, and, finally, a dessert of fresh fruit or, occasionally, a tart. The cost of these delicious meals is shared between the government and parents, who pay more or less according to their family income.

Students have about forty-five minutes for lunch, and they are encouraged to eat slowly and enjoy their meal. They eat off heated ceramic plates and use real silverware instead of disposable cutlery. Adult monitors walk around to answer questions and encourage kids to finish their food before they go outside and play.

In French lunchrooms, everything from the cutlery and decor to the tasty meals promotes an appreciation of food. Schoolchildren also take special taste education classes, discussing subjects that range from the anatomy of the tongue to how taste has changed through time. And every October, the entire country celebrates *La Semaine du Goût*, or "National Tasting Week," when famous chefs offer classes to children and adults alike.

1 French bread is renowned for its crackling crust and buttery lightness inside. The people of France like their bread so much that when describing something that seems endless, they say "As long as a day without bread." The late 18th-century French Revolution, which ended the rule of French kings and queens, began, in part, when poor peasants staged bread riots protesting the price increase of their most important food.

2 The French have created at least 300 different kinds of cheese, each with distinct flavors and methods of production. A mild-tasting cheese from northern France, called *Vieux Boulogne*, is considered the stinkiest in the world. A British commentator described it as having the aroma of "six-week-old earwax"!

3 Low-fat meats such as chicken are usually on the school lunch menu in France. With healthy choices available to students at a reasonable price every day, plus nutrition education built into the meal, it's no surprise that the number of overweight children in France is among the lowest in Europe.

4 To prevent kids from loading up on sugary juices, only water is served during school lunch. Vending machines selling soda pop and snacks have been banned in French schools since 2005.

Good Food for a Change
Kids Take Charge in the United States

The final straw was the experiment measuring the amount of grease they could squeeze out of their cafeteria hamburger. With a tray half full of glistening fat, the fourth graders at Madison, Wisconsin's Nuestro Mundo Community School were completely grossed out. They had to do something about the unhealthy food in their cafeteria. They wanted more fresh fruit and vegetables, less disposable packing, and lunches that reflect the diverse cultures in the community, such as rice and beans or Chinese noodle soup.

So in spring 2009, they formed a group called Boycott School Lunch (BCSL). Then they decided to show the school and their classmates exactly what a healthy lunch looks like by hosting a peaceful protest picnic. They planned to lay out tablecloths, arrange flowers, and get everyone to bring in potluck dishes to eat together.

But the school board—citing concerns about allergies and media attention—asked the kids to cancel their picnic. BCSL reluctantly agreed, although it didn't stop its healthy food protest. The students launched a letter-writing campaign and continued to pressure the board for changes to the menu. When school opened again in the fall, the cafeteria food had improved a bit, and, by October, the board had announced plans to make big changes to food services—a major victory for these fourth-grade activists.

Kids at Nuestro Mundo aren't the only ones objecting to unhealthy school lunch. Student-led boycotts, Facebook petitions, and other peaceful demonstrations have popped up as kids begin to see the effects—on them and on their environment—of the highly processed junk food available in so many cafeterias. Schools, teachers, and politicians are being forced to pay attention. Who says kids don't want healthy food!

Farm to School
Going Back to the Land in Italy

When children at a school in Budoia, a tiny town in northern Italy, discovered the cabbage in their school lunch came from the Netherlands, they were confused. After all, Italy is home to some of the best food and farmland in the world—why eat cabbage from somewhere else? Kids and their parents started asking questions and found the lunches were supplied by a multinational company that bought food from all over the globe. With the support of the school and town council, the kids and their families began to revamp lunch with an emphasis on buying from organic farmers in the area.

Today, a local co-op runs the kitchen, and parents help order the food—cheese, pasta, olive oil, produce—ahead of time. This means the region's sustainable food producers have a guaranteed buyer. It's a winning arrangement: The school supports environmentally friendly farmers; Budoia's economy benefits because the farmers are thriving; and the kids get great-tasting, local, organic food. It's so delicious that staff members at town council now have their lunch prepared at the school canteen!

Mexico City, Mexico

It's noon and time for *almuerzo* [ahl-**mwhere**-soh], a small lunch or snack, at this Mexico City school. Kids race outside to sit at tables set up in the concrete playground area. There is no meal program, so most students eat food from home. After school, in mid-afternoon, the family will share their main meal of the day together.

Mothers gather at the school's big iron gates to pass their children's *almuerzo* through the bars. Other kids have brought a light meal—fruit, a flavored drink, a sandwich known as *tortas* [**tor**-tahs] or a taco—from home. Some snack vendors are allowed to come inside the gates, but many others stay just outside school property.

Children sometimes buy a skewer of sweet mango or maybe a cup of chopped fruit sprinkled with chili powder and salt. But snacks such as chips and soft drinks are the most popular.

Recently, vendors who come inside the school gates have been banned from offering candy, soda pop, and high-fat snacks. It's part of a government attempt to combat rising rates of obesity. One-third of the kids on the playground are overweight or obese. (Seventy percent of their parents are, too.)

As the country has developed and more people have moved to cities to find work, Mexicans have abandoned their healthy traditional diet of corn and beans for high-fat, high-sugar convenience foods. These unhealthy foods are often the cheapest, too. Orange soda pop is less expensive than real orange juice, and pizza is half the price of a fresh salad.

1 On average, Mexicans drink 159 L (42 U.S. gal) of soft drinks per year—enough to fill an oil barrel. In 2006, a proposed tax on soda was quashed when Mexican politicians claimed it punished the poor (who tend to consume the cheap drink the most).

2 *Frijoles* [free-**hole**-lays], or beans, are a Mexican staple and are often the only thing the poorest families have to eat. To help them, the government offers money to parents with low incomes who keep their kids in school. Still, 1 in 25 kids in Mexico City drops out before they are 15 years old, often working to help their families.

3 Chips are popular, but toasted grasshoppers are also considered a treat in the state of Oaxaca. Called *chapulines* [chap-oh-**lean**-ays], they're cooked with lemon juice, salt, and garlic or hot chilies. According to a United Nations report, eating insects is good for your health (they're full of protein) and the environment! Bugs are plentiful and live in the wild, so there's no need for forests to be destroyed for farmland.

4 All over the world, processed snacks such as chips are cheaper than whole foods. Fresh products go bad quickly, so they are more expensive to store and transport. But it is also because farmers growing the basic ingredients of these processed foods—things like corn and soybeans (called commodity crops)—are heavily subsidized by governments. As a result, corn can be sold for very little and turned into products like the sweetener high-fructose corn syrup—present in almost everything we eat, from ketchup to soda, breakfast cereal to chips.

Dadaab Refugee Camps, Kenya

Dust and sand gets into everything at this school in the Dadaab refugee camps near the Kenya–Somalia border. There are one hundred children in each sweltering, tin-walled classroom, and six kids must share a single desk and textbook. Classes are organized in shifts to accommodate more kids.

When lunch arrives, the children line up with plastic mugs to receive hot porridge supplied by the World Food Programme (WFP). A group of parents ladle the nutrient-fortified corn–soy blend (known as CSB) out of massive pots; often it is so thin the children can drink the sweet, nutty-tasting mush while they squat on the ground outside the school.

Most of the people in Dadaab are Somali refugees. Refugees are people who have fled their homelands because they are no longer safe. Some Somali families have been in Dadaab since the early 1990s after a civil war tore their country apart. Today, violence continues in Somalia, and more than four hundred and fifty thousand people have sought refuge at Dadaab, cramming into an area intended for ninety thousand.

Half of the residents of Dadaab are under seventeen years old. Education is free, and the school meal has helped increase attendance. But half the kids still don't go. For some, it is because the schools are overcrowded and lack resources. Others must work for their families.

With an inadequate water supply, little electricity, few sanitation facilities, and homes made from tin and tarps, life is a constant struggle. Getting proper food to eat is one of the biggest challenges. With no land to grow food, refugees must rely on school feeding and twice-a-month WFP food rations.

1 The World Food Programme (WFP) is a United Nations agency. It feeds more than 90 million hungry people in more than 70 countries around the world. Every year, it ships almost four million tons of food to nations in crisis. In Dadaab, sometimes a flood or an outbreak of disease makes it impossible to safely make porridge, so WFP offers children high-energy biscuits enriched with protein and nutrients instead.

2 Some fresh fruit and vegetables are available in the informal markets in Dadaab. But most people have no money to buy them. With support from international organizations, some vulnerable women (single parents, the elderly, women with HIV/AIDS) have planted multi-tiered gardens using empty grain bags and recycled oilcans. The gardens require little soil and use only wastewater for growing. The women plant vegetables such as tomatoes, okra, leafy greens, and eggplant to add much-needed nutrients to their family's diet.

3 Since most Somalis are Muslim, food in Dadaab must be halal, which means it meets strict religious guidelines. The porridge and other WFP rations are considered halal because they are vegetarian. Traditional foods from Somalia include richly spiced dishes using halal lamb, goat, and camel meat. Because Italy controlled parts of Somalia for more than 50 years, spaghetti is also a common Somali dish.

4 Dadaab's growing population is outpacing its crumbling water system. The camps can provide only about 17 L (4.5 U.S. gal.) of water per person per day—below the United Nations minimum standard of 20 L (5.3 U.S. gal.) that is needed to maintain good health.

Toronto, Canada

A loud bell sounds through the school in downtown Toronto, Canada's largest city. Kids grab their lunch bags and head to the gymnasium to eat. The gym is small and airless, smelling mildly of sweat and running shoes. There isn't a special lunchroom, so every day this space gets turned into an eating area with collapsible tables. At other schools, kids sit on the floor or eat at their desks. Most children bring their meals from home, packed in lunch boxes, thermoses, and plastic bags.

Some schools provide breakfast or a snack; others offer a meal. Even in a wealthy city such as Toronto, one in four children lives in poverty, and ninety thousand kids rely on these free food programs to make it through the day. But the programs exist only because of volunteer efforts and a patchwork of funding from local governments, school boards and businesses. Canada is one of the few developed nations in the world that doesn't offer a national nutrition program for school-age children.

In this noisy, crowded gymnasium, there are as many different kinds of lunches as there are children. Canada is a nation of immigrants. One out of every five people was born in another country. Rice and beans, curries, sushi, and noodle soups all turn up in the kids' lunch boxes, though sandwiches are most common.

When the children have finished their meal, students in the eco-club help their classmates sort through the garbage they produce. Uneaten food such as apple cores and bread crusts goes into a green bin. It will be composted and used in the school garden. Paper and plastic packaging can be recycled or thrown out. Every year, the average Canadian kid produces 30 kg (66 lbs.) of garbage just from lunches—that's about the weight of a ten-year-old boy!

1 Everyone enjoys a sweet treat sometimes! But some snacks are loaded with fat and sugar. These mini cookies have 200 calories a pack, about the same amount as a small steak. In Canada, one out of four kids is overweight or obese.

2 Kids like packaged snacks because they are quick and easy to eat. But some educators don't think children should be eating so fast. A number of schools in western Canada have come up with a solution: play first, eat later. Teachers say kids focus less on rushing through their lunch and more on enjoying their meal.

3 These baby carrots aren't "babies" at all. They're the invention of a California farmer tired of throwing out twisted or imperfect-looking carrots. "Baby-cut" carrots are simply regular ones chopped and whittled into shape. They're still tasty and good for you. Carrots are a great source of beta-carotene, which is essential for healthy eyesight.

4 Canadian school boards make hundreds of thousands of dollars a year through vending machine contracts with drink and snack companies. Health experts have fought to fill these machines—often loaded with sugary soda pop and snacks—with healthier choices. But it's a hard sell; cash-strapped school boards fear losing money. Recently, however, some of Canada's largest provinces have banned junk food from schools—a hopeful sign for the future.

Belo Horizonte, Brazil

The smell of rice and beans fills the cafeteria as lunchtime begins at this school in Belo Horizonte, an industrial city in southeastern Brazil. Children come and go—each class has a specific time slot for eating. The hot meal is free for all public school kids in Brazil. For some, especially children living in the remote and poverty-stricken rural northeast, it is their main meal of the day.

Brazil is the largest country in Latin America. Despite a growing economy, it is still one of the most unequal nations in the world. That means the difference between the richest people and the poorest is very big. Nearly forty-two million Brazilians (more than the entire population of Canada) live in poverty and are unable to afford adequate food or shelter.

In 2002, Brazil elected a president whom everyone called Lula. He had grown up poor and worked as a shoeshine boy as a child. One of the first things Lula did in government was commit to fighting hunger and inequality in Brazil. School lunch is one of many programs aimed at getting healthy food to hungry people.

Meals are served on colorful plates. There is always rice and beans, plus grilled beef or chicken with potatoes or kale and either fresh fruit or juice. The cooks try to use what's in season, so native fruits such as pineapple, bananas, and guava often show up on the menu.

The free school lunch and other food programs in Brazil have proved amazingly successful at decreasing poverty and hunger. Since 2003, child malnutrition has been reduced by 73% and the number of people living in poverty has been cut in half.

1 As international demand for Brazilian beef has risen in the last decade, deforestation of the vital Amazon rain forest has increased. The Amazon, in the north of Brazil, is the largest and most species-rich tropical rain forest in the world. Environmentalists have been working for decades to defend it. Deforestation of rain forests is responsible for 17% of all greenhouse gas emissions around the world.

2 Most Brazilians eat rice and beans—a complete protein when eaten together—at least once a day. Sometimes manioc flour is sprinkled on top. Made from the root of the manioc plant (also known as yucca or cassava), it adds a nutty flavor and texture to the dish.

4 School lunch often includes drinks such as passion fruit juice. Vendors selling soda pop (plus candy and other treats) have been banned from schools in Belo Horizonte. But fast-food companies are still reaching kids in other ways, including promoting unhealthy products on some Brazilian TV networks and the Internet.

3 Brazil is one of the main banana-producing nations on the planet. Most of the fruit grown here is eaten in the country. Schools in Brazil are required to buy a portion of lunch ingredients from local producers; this supports farmers and cuts down on storage, processing, and transportation. Connecting the dots between schools and farms and between education and the economy has been at the root of the successful change in Brazil's food system.

Life Lessons

Fighting for Food Justice in Canada

Toronto, Canada

Sunlight filters through the massive windows as fifth graders file into The Stop Community Food Centre's Green Barn. A once-derelict building in downtown Toronto, it's been transformed into a sustainable food production and education center with lush gardens, a greenhouse, and a professional kitchen. Kids come to learn about growing, cooking, and eating good food; they also learn how what they eat is connected to health, the environment, and social justice.

The students start by planting tomato seedlings in the greenhouse, and then move inside to play The Game of Real Life. Each person is given a role and pretend money to spend. One girl is a wealthy character. She's excited to buy a big house, toys, and good food. Someone else is assigned a character in a wheelchair; others live on minimum wage or government welfare. Those on low incomes discover that after paying rent they have little to spend on healthy meals. Some must use food banks. One boy's character gets sick because the cheap food that fits in his budget is full of fat, sugar, and salt. The noise level rises—all the kids agree that this isn't fair.

Afterwards, the class does an exercise in which students imagine they are politicians deciding on solutions that make sense. Should the minimum wage be increased? Would more community gardens help? The students debate and discuss it all.

The program asks kids to think about food justice so they will begin to see their own roles in helping to both protect the planet and question inequality. The fifth graders leave the workshop excited about changing their own eating habits and about pushing for social change. Back in class, the first thing on the agenda is writing a letter to their political representative. These kids know exactly what they want: healthy food for everyone!

Water World
A Floating School Garden in Bangladesh

The wooden boat glides up to a muddy embankment in Singra, a village in northwestern Bangladesh. A long plank is extended to the ground and the waiting children eagerly step on board their floating school.

Run on solar power and towing a floating garden, this boat and seventeen others are part classroom, part veggie patch, all innovation. Without the boats, many poor kids would go without education and fresh produce when their schools and fields are flooded or destroyed during the annual rainy season. The gardens, built on floating beds of water hyacinth and bamboo, are tended by parents who share the eggplant, spinach, and sweet gourds grown there.

Flooding has always been a problem in Bangladesh. But global warming has melted the Himalayan glaciers that feed its many rivers, and floods have become more severe. Entire villages have disappeared under water, and scientists predict more low-lying land will be submerged as the melting continues.

This is the frontline of climate change. Bangladeshis hope that ingenious ideas such as these floating classrooms will help them meet the challenges of a changing world.

Dubna, Russia

The hallway is noisy and packed with children headed for lunch at this school in Dubna, a riverside city in western Russia. The cafeteria is a large room on the first floor, and it fills up quickly. Most Russian students eat at school because the food there is inexpensive.

Traditionally, *obed* [ah-**bed**] is the main meal of the day, and even at school the food is hearty. The cafeteria offers soup followed by a beef or fish main course with mashed potatoes or *kasha*, a kind of porridge. Kids can each pick up a slice or two of bread and include a sweet fruit drink on their trays.

Russia was once part of a huge country called the Soviet Union, which dissolved into fifteen separate nations in the early 1990s. Food shortages were common during the Soviet period. People stood in long lineups simply to buy their daily bread. During this time, the Russian government encouraged people to eat meat, fat, and bread, paying less attention to fresh vegetables and fruits.

Eating habits have changed since then, but 20% of school-aged kids remain malnourished. Some students don't have enough, while others don't receive proper nutrients from the foods they eat. As a result, children in Russia's poorest regions are shorter on average than kids elsewhere in the world. And heart disease—linked to poor nutrition and the cause of 52% of adult deaths in the country—is on the rise among young people.

Hoping to promote healthier eating habits, officials in Russia have banned junk food and soda pop in schools. Teachers walk around the cafeteria at lunch to ensure kids are eating well. Children also take lessons in table manners, learning how to properly hold their knives and forks and how to set the table.

1 This healthy and colorful soup, called *borsch*, is a Russian favorite eaten hot or cold. Beets give the soup its strong color. These root vegetables are packed with fiber and are a rich source of other nutrients. Health experts often recommend choosing food with bright colors—such as the red of beets or the deep blue of blueberries—because the colors are clues to their health-giving punch.

2 *Kasha* is a porridge made of toasted buckwheat or other cereals such as oatmeal. It's been part of the Russian diet for centuries. "Cabbage soup and *kasha* are all we need to live on," an old proverb claims. But Russians today would probably also include bread—the average person eats about 60 kg (132 lbs.) of it every year!

3 Saltshakers are placed on the tables in the school cafeteria. In most developed countries, iodine is added to table salt because it's an easy way to consume the essential micronutrient. But this is not always the case in Russia. As a result, about 40% of children have iodine deficiency, which can result in a loss of learning ability.

4 This delicious fruit drink, called compote, is made by boiling fruits such as apples, dried prunes, or raisins with sugar and water. There are usually chunks of fruit left in the bottom of the glass that you can eat with a spoon!

Cusco, Peru

Every morning, the children from this community in the Peruvian Andes outside Cusco walk two hours over rough roads to get to school. Like many small mountain schools, there is limited electricity and no running water.

Mid-morning, the children lay out cloths and share a snack called *qoqaw* [**ko**-kow], or "traveler's food," they have brought from home. There is roasted maize (corn) served cold and, on special occasions, a dry salty cheese to eat with it.

The children here are Quechua [**Ke**-chew-ah], people native to the Andes with a unique language and culture. Their families are *campesinos* [camp-eh-**see**-nos], or "peasant farmers," who plant and tend hilly plots growing potatoes, corn, and beans.

In the past, Quechua farmers cultivated a great variety of each species—many different kinds of potatoes, for instance—to ensure a strong harvest. But during the last fifty years, the diversity of food crops has decreased dramatically, making farmers vulnerable to weather and pests. The World Food Programme reports that up to 70% of children in Peru's most isolated regions are chronically undernourished.

Just after noon, the kids return home, traveling the same long path they took in the morning. Because their parents are working on the family land, children prepare their own food for lunch. It is the main meal of the day and nearly always includes potatoes. The children eat with their siblings before helping their parents in the fields or at home.

Most of these families do not have a lot of money. Nearly 40% of Peruvians live on less than $1.25 (U.S.) a day. Strong community and cultural networks allow the Quechua people to survive and thrive in this mountainous land.

1 Potatoes originally come from Peru, where some 3500 kinds are grown, including yellow, red, blue, purple, spotted, twisted, hooked, and knobbly types. Easy to grow and boasting a wide variety of tastes and textures (from smooth to waxy, bland to sweet), these potatoes are also a good source of energy, vitamins, and micronutrients. The average Peruvian eats about 530 potatoes every year!

2 Maize (corn) is a staple food grown in Peru, the main ingredient in everything from tamales to beer. It is often used in dishes prepared at the country's many "community kitchens," where local produce is preferred to imported foods. Run by women in largely urban neighborhoods, these kitchens provide healthy and affordable meals to hundreds of thousands of poor families. They have also become key centers for community organizing and protest.

3 Guinea pigs or *cuy* (pronounced **koo**-*ee* in Spanish for the sound they make) are a favorite pet in North America. But in Peru, the Quechua people have been raising the animals for food and medicine since the time of the Inca between the 13th and 16th centuries. Fried, roasted, or boiled whole, they taste like rabbit and are an important source of protein and iron.

4 *Quinoa* [**keen**-wah], a seed grown in the Andes, was considered sacred by the Inca. It's now thought to be one of the most nutritious foods on the planet. Quinoa is full of fiber and rich in protein, which allows your body to build and repair muscle. Nutty and earthy tasting, it's eaten as porridge or served hot like rice and mixed with spices and vegetables.

Roswell, United States

Lunch ladies stand behind the counter wearing hairnets and plastic white aprons, the day's offerings under heat lamps in front of them. This school in central New Mexico doesn't have a suitable kitchen for cooking, so the staff must reheat frozen and canned food for the government-subsidized meal.

More than half the kids in the lineup pay nothing or a very small amount for their hot lunch because their family income is low. Those who can afford it pay between two and three dollars (U.S.) a day or bring a packed lunch from home.

There is always a main dish such as pizza or tacos, plus fruit, a vegetable, and a choice between chocolate, strawberry or regular milk. Kids with some pocket change can add extra items such as cookies or more pizza to their trays.

More than thirty-one million kids eat school lunch every day in the U.S. But some of the meals aren't as nutritious as they could be. Over the last three decades, obesity rates among American children have tripled. Along with excessive weight gain comes serious health problems such as type 2 diabetes.

Parents, teachers and food activists have been working to change school lunch for many years. They've introduced salad bars, built better kitchen facilities, and created local buying policies. One example is the Edible Schoolyard in Berkeley, California. There, kids plant and grow food in the school garden and then cook it in their kitchen classroom. There are many promising projects, but if current levels of poor health continue, American children will have a lower life expectancy than their parents' generation.

1 Brand name food such as Domino's Pizza and KFC are sold at more than one-third of U.S. public schools. According to a study funded by the National Institutes of Health, a ban on marketing unhealthy foods to children would reduce the number of overweight kids by up to 18%.

2 Most of the milk Americans drink comes from cows, but throughout history, nearly every kind of livestock species—including horses, camels, buffalo, and yak—has provided drinking milk for humans. Today, Americans consume about 84 L (22 gal.) of milk per person per year—that's enough to fill a bathtub!

3 Eaten straight off the cob or in a fresh salad, corn can be a great addition to any meal. But most of the 10 million bushels of corn grown in the U.S. each year is turned into animal feed, biofuel, and food additives such as the sweetener high-fructose corn syrup (HFCS). HFCS is so cheap and plentiful in processed foods that the average American consumes about 17 kg (37.5 lbs.) of it per year.

4 The fruit in U.S. school lunches often comes from a can, but more and more schools are offering fresh fruit and vegetables as part of Farm to School programs. These programs not only connect kids with local farmers, they bring fresh, local produce to the schools, offer opportunities to learn about the environment, and support sustainable agriculture.

Kandahar, Afghanistan

This village school outside Kandahar city in Afghanistan's southern province used to be little more than a makeshift tent with thick fabric draped over wooden poles stuck in the hard-packed red earth. After decades of war and violence, the building has finally been reconstructed with brick walls, but there are not enough desks or books for each student, no safe drinking water or proper toilet facilities. Some children do their lessons sitting on traditional rugs on the ground.

At midday, the teacher stops the class for a meal of high-energy biscuits provided by the World Food Programme (WFP). Students eat sitting on the rugs, which is traditional in Afghan culture.

The biscuits are a cross between cookies and crackers. They're made of wheat and fortified with vitamins, minerals, and protein. Each 100 g (3.5 oz.) package of ten to fifteen biscuits provides four hundred and fifty calories—the energy equivalent of a skinless chicken breast with two cups of broccoli. For many kids, the biscuits are both breakfast and lunch and the most nutritious food they will have all day.

Afghanistan was once considered an agricultural powerhouse. But today, 54% of young Afghan children don't have enough to eat, and more than half the population lives on less than one dollar (U.S.) a day.

School is a haven from this difficult life—especially for girls. Between 1996 and 2001, when the radical Taliban government was in power, girls were banned from going to school. Even now, only one-third of students are girls. As added encouragement for families to send them to school, girls receive an extra cooking oil ration from WFP to take home. But in areas where the Taliban remains active, girls still risk their lives simply by walking to school.

1 The biscuits are supplied by the World Food Programme. The WFP supports nearly two million Afghan children through its food-for-education programs— boosting attendance by offering food. It has recently begun providing hot meals in some schools. Those kids receive a dish of split peas fortified with micronutrient powder, and bread on the side.

2 Girls who attend school a minimum of 22 days a month receive a 4.5 kg (10 lb.) tin of cooking oil. It will be used by the student's family to make tasty flat breads and to fry onions, veggies, and meat (usually lamb or beef) for traditional Afghan dishes such as *qorma* [**core**-ma], a stew served with rice. When the oil tin is empty, the metal is often recycled; people use it to make everything from mini-barbecues to toy cars, even small guitars.

1

2

3

3 Over one year, wheat prices rose 60% in Afghanistan. Around the world, prices for basic food staples have risen to the point that we face a serious food crisis. There are many reasons, including economic turmoil, high oil prices, and poor growing seasons due to climate change. Fewer farmers are growing food because they have moved to biofuel production—growing corn, wheat, and soy to be made into fuel. The result is less available food grains and skyrocketing prices, leaving the poorest people in the world more vulnerable to hunger than ever before.

A Cultural Revolution
Reclaiming Ancient Wisdom in Peru

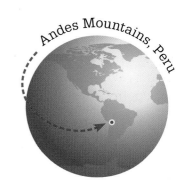

Andes Mountains, Peru

It's corn harvest time at the school *chacra* [**chahk**-rah], Quechua for "field," high in the Andes mountains of southern Peru. The children, who tend the small rocky strip of land to grow corn and potatoes, are excited. The whole village has come out to celebrate. They follow the traditional customs, first burning incense and coca leaves, showing respect to Mother Earth. Then, when it's time to harvest, the elders ask permission of the local gods, and while they cut the corn, everyone sings. Later, the community eats together, thanking the gods for the bounty.

Such celebrations have been going on for generations in these highlands. But until recently, Peruvian teachers and school administrators discouraged traditional culture in schools. School was for reading, writing, and arithmetic—in Spanish. Quechua-speaking children simply had to struggle through, learning to be ashamed of their language and way of life.

But reforms to the education system and innovative local projects have reintroduced traditional knowledge as part of the curriculum in some schools. Modern education isn't ignored, but it is only a part of what is taught. They call this approach *Iskay Yachay* [**Ees**-kai **Yah**-chai] in Quechua, meaning two kinds of knowledge.

Since most families in the mountains are farmers, teachers make time for the rituals and cycles of planting, allowing kids time off to help in the fields. Elders are also invited to share their knowledge of plants, native medicines, and farming techniques at school seed fairs and garden celebrations. Kids learn Andean poetry, art, and music. They also plant and tend the school *chacra*, growing food for both themselves and their community, preparing to be future caretakers of Mother Earth.

The Global Garden
Growing Food and Community around the World

Whether growing or eating it, food has a way of bringing people together. That's something children at three hundred schools in Kenya, India, Singapore, the Gambia, the U.S., and Britain have discovered firsthand in a global network called Gardens for Life.

Through specially designed teaching and learning resources, plus a website, Gardens for Life (part of the U.K.-based Eden Project) connects kids around the world who are growing food at school.

In Kenya's drought-prone Rift Valley, sixty schools are involved. Years of failed crops and the rising cost of food staples has made school lunch too expensive for many poor families. But by cultivating school land, students are growing vegetables such as spinach and eggplant for their meals. Now kids get nutritious lunches, plus learn farming skills. And any extra produce is sold to raise money for the classrooms.

Every school in the Gardens for Life network has a story. By sharing them, kids are challenged to consider how food connects them to one another and to worldwide issues such as sustainability and poverty. The Gardens for Life children and their teachers are truly building a community of global citizens—one veggie at a time.

Birmingham, England

A few years ago, England's school dinner (as the noonday meal is called) looked a lot different. Hamburgers, french fries, fizzy drinks, and Turkey Twizzlers were all on the menu in school canteens. (Turkey Twizzlers are deep-fried spiral strips of processed turkey mixed with pork fat!)

But then staggering numbers emerged showing England was the most obese country in Europe, with about one-quarter of kids between two and fifteen years old overweight or obese. Parents and food activists—including celebrity chef Jamie Oliver, who hosted a popular TV program about school dinner—convinced the government to alter the noonday meal.

Today, the kids lining up in this small community school outside Birmingham are served a healthy meal (with a vegetarian option). By law, English school kitchens must not sell deep-fried foods more than twice a week. Saltshakers, chocolate bars, and soda pop are all banned. Students are offered at least two servings of fruit and vegetables every day and high-quality meat on a regular basis.

At first, many kids rejected the healthy food. One group of parents in the city of Rotherham protested by passing burgers and fish and chips through the locked gates of their children's school!

But kids and their families are starting to embrace the new lunches. At this Birmingham school, children have planted a fruit and vegetable garden to add to their meals, and they take regular field

trips to local farms. The students even chose colorful cloths to be laid on the tables during lunch. When healthy food is combined with a more relaxed environment, children's behavior improves in both the canteen and the classroom. Teachers say that students can concentrate better and actually focus on doing their work.

1 Carrots are England's second favorite vegetable (potatoes top the list). Most carrots today are grown in the country and bought at supermarkets. Food activists call the distance food must journey from field to fork *food miles*—counting them to show the environmental impact of what we eat. A British carrot today travels 60% more food miles than a carrot would have traveled in the 1970s. But food miles aren't the only way food affects the environment. Growing, processing, and storing food also contribute to greenhouse gas emissions.

2 In a recent survey, children and parents chose this classic British meal as their favorite school dinner. Traditionally served on Sundays, it features roast beef in gravy and is served with sides. Sausage (known as bangers) with mashed potatoes and onion gravy came second in the survey, followed by lasagna with garlic bread.

3 Yorkshire pudding, a puffy cooked pastry, was originally served as a cheap side dish to make roast dinner more filling for the poor. Today, low-income students receive school dinner for free. But many eligible kids are ashamed to be seen "on free dinners." New systems, such as having all students use automated lunch cards, are being tested to overcome prejudices. Even more promising are pilot projects offering free, healthy meals to *all* the kids in the canteen.

Shanghai, China

The kids in this busy Shanghai school cafeteria are hungry. They've been at school since 7:30 a.m. when their first lesson began, and they'll stay there for nearly nine hours. China is the most populous country in the world, more than a billion strong. Education is very important, and the pressure to do well is intense.

In the cafeteria, a big room with long tables, the students collect their lunch—usually rice or noodles, pork or fish, and vegetables, with soup on the side. The kids rarely have cold drinks with their food because traditional Chinese medicine considers cold liquids with a hot meal bad for digestion.

Teachers stroll around the cafeteria, encouraging children not to be too noisy and to chew their food carefully. Teachers command respect and obedience from the kids—after all, it's the law in China! When lunch is finished, some kids head outside while others return to the classroom to grab a quick nap or study some more.

Today, 15% of ten to twelve year olds living in China's cities are overweight, and another 8% are obese. Some people blame this sharp rise in obesity on too much studying and not enough physical activity. It also reflects wider changes in the Chinese lifestyle. A booming economy has pushed people from rural areas into cities. There, they are less active and eat more meat, dairy, and Western-style fast food such as the popular KFC.

To combat obesity, compulsory folk dancing classes have been introduced at some schools; elsewhere, provincial governments require students to run 1 km (0.6 mi.) a day during their breaks.

1 Over the last two centuries, the failure of the Chinese rice crop has caused serious famines (most recently in the 1950s and 1960s), with tens of millions of people starving to death. As a result, being plump became a sign of good health and wealth—something health experts are now working hard to change. Still, some people continue to use the old saying: "A fat child is a healthy child."

1

3 In northern China, making slurping noises when drinking hot soup or eating noodles is not just acceptable, it's considered polite! Sucking in air cools the hot liquid and shows appreciation for the food.

2 Since the mid-1980s, consumption of meat has more than doubled in China. If this trend continues—and the Chinese economy and population continue to grow—it will have huge environmental consequences. Meat production is hard on Earth. Land must be cleared for pastures and feed crops, and animals produce large amounts of greenhouse gases that contribute to climate change. Getting rid of their waste in an ecologically friendly way (not polluting water sources, especially) is also very difficult.

4 The southern Chinese diet has traditionally focused on rice and vegetables such as the bok choy in this dish. (The leafy greens taste like sweet cabbage.) Chefs try to prepare meals that appeal to all the senses, so vegetables are cooked very quickly to retain their flavor, bright color, and texture.

The Power of Food

This book is about school lunch, but it's also about the international food system—a system not unlike the human body with many moving and interconnected parts. For instance, it's impossible to talk about food in any depth without also touching on the plight of farmers, the challenges of world hunger, equality, diet-related illnesses, or the impact on the environment.

Each school lunch you've read about acts like a lens, magnifying, clarifying, sometimes even complicating these issues. And despite the disparate experiences of children around the world, some important themes emerge.

Fast-Food Culture

Everywhere we go, children and adults are bombarded with images and words selling unhealthy, preservative-laden, processed foods. They're on TV and the Internet, in movies and video games, on the streets, and even in schools. The power and reach of the international corporations who make these products are astonishing. Fast food has become our shared global culture.

Nutrition Transition

As the influence of this culture has grown, and countries have become more urban and prosperous, people are abandoning their traditional diets in favor of meat, dairy products, and processed food. Experts call this the nutrition transition. The result is the obesity crisis, among other things—and a new kind of malnutrition that comes from eating too much food with not enough nutrients.

Buying Global

All these changes are made possible because of technological innovations. Fifty years ago, you wouldn't find strawberries in a Canadian lunch box in February, and you wouldn't eat Brazilian beef if you lived in Japan. But the post–World War II revolution in food production has transformed what we eat. Small-scale farms have been replaced with machinery, fertilizers, pesticides, and scientifically engineered seeds. Global transportation systems offer both speed and refrigeration. Add to this artificial additives and preservatives, and we've built a system based on eating whatever we want when we want it.

The Consequences of Convenience

Shifts so enormous are never without consequences. In country after country, we see the health impact of these changes in increased obesity, malnourishment, and diet-related illnesses.

The rise of this fuel-intensive, international food system has also tipped the global balance of power even more toward developed nations. The global poor—more than a billion strong, their numbers concentrated in the developing world—benefit least. Their vulnerability (the absence of what activists call food security), in fact, has increased as economic turmoil and rising prices for staples such as wheat, corn, and rice have caused a global food crisis.

Another major impact of this food system is on the environment—from the vast amounts of packaging and food waste produced at Canadian schools every lunchtime to the deforestation of the Amazon rain forest in favor of beef cattle ranches. According to the United Nation's Food and Agriculture Organization, the livestock sector alone contributes to 18% of worldwide greenhouse gas emissions.

Reclaiming School Lunch

The good news is, in schools from France to Peru and school gardens from Kenya to America, students and adults are reclaiming school lunch and the food system. They are demanding more nutritious cafeteria options and fighting to ban junk-food advertising. They're planting gardens, creating eco-clubs to cut down on waste, and learning how to cook healthy meals. They are insisting that some of the food sold in school cafeterias is sourced locally. They're arguing that food is more than a mere commodity on the world market and that everyone deserves to eat healthily. At its best, how we eat, grow, and share our meals is a celebration of tradition and history, of cultural heritage, and of community.

Kids Can Change the Food System

School lunch is an ideal opportunity for parents and teachers to help children see the impact they can have on the world, to see themselves as people able to make change. Eating lunch at school is something kids do every day. We can all try to "vote with our fork" and choose foods that are healthy for us and Earth.

Adults can also help children make connections between these individual decisions, the community, and the world. We can encourage kids to speak out about hunger and poverty at home and abroad, advocating for school feeding programs to help the chronically hungry. These programs do so much more than just fill bellies: They increase attendance (especially of girls) and improve behavior and learning capabilities.

Kids need to know that as citizens of their schools and communities, they can advocate—to education administrators and politicians—for policies that ensure access to healthy food in general, and to school lunch in particular, is a basic human right.

Food is a powerful tool, and one that everyone can use, no matter how young. It can build communities, challenge inequalities, and break down barriers between people.

Food really does connect us all.

Here are some ways you and your class can get involved in making positive changes to our food system.

Plant a school food garden.

Learn how fruit, vegetables, and herbs grow. Reclaim traditions in your community. Learn about the challenges of eating fresh produce on a low income. Collect waste and build a composter for lunch scraps. Recycle packaging. Encourage kids to bring litterless lunches to school.

Host a food festival.

Invite local food producers and people from your community to share favorite dishes from their culture. Have tastings and a cooking contest. Share seeds or seedlings so people can grow plants on their balconies and backyards. Visit a farmers' market and buy locally produced food.

Give testimony at your local government.

Write letters to your political representatives asking them to support healthy food and local procurement policies in schools. Raise your concerns about the impact of the industrial food system on your environment. Tell them you think it's not right that vulnerable people in your neighborhood can't afford to eat properly. Ask them to write back!

Educate yourself about where your food comes from.

Ask questions about who grows or makes your food, how workers are treated, whether they use pesticides or fertilizers, and how those chemicals break down in the air, soil and water. Follow one tomato, potato, or other plant from seed to table. Find out what percentage of your school meal comes from your region. Calculate the food miles and other environmental costs of your lunch.

Glossary

additive: something added to food to change it; for example, to make it sweeter

biofuel: fuel made from plant matter such as corn, soy, or wheat

boycott: to refuse to buy or take part in something because you disagree with it

calories: a measurement of the amount of energy provided by food

climate change: a change in weather around the world; especially refers to the warming of Earth

co-op: a store, group, or organization in which all members own shares and participate in running it

commodity crops: unprocessed or partially processed food products such as soybeans and corn, the basic price of which is set by global markets

deficiency: the state of lacking something necessary, especially nutrients such as iron (as in anemia) or iodine (as in iodine deficiency)

deforestation: the cutting down of forests; refers especially to the rain forest being cut down for cattle pastures

developed nation: a relatively wealthy and technologically advanced country in which most people's basic needs (food, shelter, education, health care, and income) are met

developing nation: a low- or middle-income country where there are fewer resources to meet people's basic needs

diabetes: a disease in which there is too much sugar in the blood; type 2 diabetes is often considered diet-related

fiber: a part of certain foods such as grains and fruit that helps the body digest

food justice: the idea that food should be a basic human right and that society should organize itself so everyone has enough food to be healthy

food miles: the distance food must travel from field to table—calculated to show the environmental, social, and economic impact of what we eat

food security: refers to the availability of food, as well as access to it

fortified: to enrich food with nutrients such as vitamins, minerals, or protein

greenhouse gas: gases such as carbon dioxide and methane that are produced on Earth and collect in the atmosphere, contributing to the warming of Earth

local: refers to food grown or produced near where you live

low income: used to describe someone who earns or receives very little money on a regular basis

malnutrition: a serious condition caused by not having enough food or by having food that is not healthy. Similar to

undernourished, which describes the state of being weak and unhealthy because of a lack of nutritious food.

nutrient: something people need to consume to stay healthy, such as protein, minerals, and vitamins. Micronutrients are essential nutrients needed in very small amounts.

obesity: the medical condition of being very overweight

organic: food that is produced without the use of chemicals or pesticides

poverty: the state of being poor, lacking food, shelter, education, and income. In the developing world, poverty refers to those living on less than $1.25 (U.S.) per day.

preservative: something used to keep food from spoiling, especially a chemical

processed food: food that has been treated, changed, or prepared in some manner so it can be easily packaged, stored, and transported

protein: a necessary nutrient required by the body for growth, repair, and maintenance of all cells

ration: a specific, limited amount of food distributed to people in emergency situations

staple: a main food item of a nation's diet

subsidize: governments contributing money, for example, to help make school lunch affordable and accessible to students

sustainable: able to be continued over the long term with minimal impact on the environment

United Nations (UN): an international organization committed to peace, security, and supporting better living standards, human rights, and equality around the world

whole foods: foods that have not been processed or refined and have no additives. Fresh vegetables and many grains are examples of whole foods.

World Food Programme (WFP): a UN program dedicated to helping people around the world who need food assistance